The Creating Machine

Language of Success

The Creating Machine

Language of Success

This handbook was written to help people understand how to engage the Creating Machine.

The power of the spoken word, the language of success, can enable you to create and fulfill your dreams and desires.

That a person can change themselves, improve themselves, recreate themselves, control their environment, and master their own destiny is the conclusion of every mind that is wide awake to the power of right thought in constructive action. ~ Christian Larsen

Have you ever tried to learn a foreign language? The language of success can be just that, foreign.

Were you raised in an environment where you thought there was never enough…. enough attention, enough money, enough time, enough space, enough love?

That's just life. It's time to change it!

One of the greatest moments in anyone's developing experience is when they no longer try to hide from themself but determine to get acquainted with themself as they really are.
~Norman Vincent Peale

As a rule, parents do the best they know how to do, but they still come with the baggage of their parents and their parents before them.

Fortunately some have a personality that enables them to look within for the positives instead of listening to the negatives.

If you're still listening to the negatives, hopefully you'll let us share with you a few of the things we've learned about the language of success and the creating machine.

The most extensive catalog of the world's languages is found in Ethnologue (published by SIL International).

This detailed list, as of 2009, included 6,909 distinct languages. David Crystal, in the Cambridge Encyclopedia of the English Language, suggests that there must be at least a million words in language.

Words are a reflection of our thoughts. Positive words come from positive thoughts, negative words from negative thoughts. Listen to the words that come out of your mouth and you will have a good idea the direction your thoughts are facing, and as a result, your life. ~ Danea Horn, Creative Affirmations

Until you master the Language of Success, your ability to communicate your dreams and desires, so that they become a reality, is floundering in the ethereal world, la la land, your subconscious or whatever you want to call it.

Make no mistake, your dreams and desires are waiting for the right language to convert to positive energy so that what you want can come into being.

If you can conceive it, if you desire it, you can convert it into words.

Desire is the starting point of all achievement, not a hope, not a wish, but a keen pulsating desire which transcends everything.
~ Napoleon Hill

I'm sure you've at one time or another experienced an "aha" moment…a fleeting moment of understanding.

The greatest events of an age are its best thoughts. It is the nature of thought to find its way into action.
~John Bovee Dods

If you're reading this handbook you're probably still looking for the last piece of the puzzle that takes your "aha" moment from the head to the heart.

Maybe you continue to struggle to do the things you know you must do to make your creating machine work like you want it to work.

Honestly, it can be mentally exhausting.

Those brief flashes of insight, or "aha" moments, can be hard to hang onto.

Day after day you start over with the determination that today it will all fall into place.

Today, you insist, I will accomplish my quest to fully engage the creating machine. Yet tomorrow comes and you're starting over once again.

The possibilities of thought training are infinite, its consequence eternal, and yet few take the pains to direct their thinking into channels that will do them good, but instead leave all to chance. ~ Orison Swett Marden

Have you lost count of the books, emails, blogs and videos you've read, watched and heard?

All of them telling you either how, when, where, why or who has gotten it right and how you can too.

I may not be there yet, but I'm closer
than I was yesterday.
~Author Unknown

You may be so enlightened you can't sleep at night. That's a joke- but possibly pretty close to the truth.

So what's keeping you from getting it right? Join us on our journey into the Language of Success.

Come dress yourself in love,
let the journey begin.
~ Francesca da Rimini

What is the Language of Success?

It's simple.

The Language of Success is thinking and speaking the specific words that activate positive energy into motion (the creating machine) that cause your dreams and desires to be manifested in your life.

Did you get that? Read it again.

The Language of Success is thinking and speaking the specific words that activate energy into motion that cause your dreams and desires to be manifested in your life, and that, is the creating machine.

Yes, you are the boss of your dreams and desires. You are in control of putting energy into motion with the words you use.

The energy of the mind is the essence of life. ~ Aristotle

What do you want in your life?

Have you stopped and given your desires and dreams serious

thought? Have you stopped long enough to use all your senses?

Can you see what you want? Can you smell it? Can you hear it? Can you taste it? Can you touch it?

You can make it real. We have an estimated 60,000 thoughts a day. Add that to a million words in the English language and that's a lot to focus on a single outcome.

To keep it simple let's break it down into a basic mathematic statement.

The Desire Manifestation Equation:

Thoughts + words + feelings = action

Take care of your Thoughts because they become Words. Take care of your Words because they will become Actions. Take care of your Actions because they will become Habits. Take care of your Habits because they will form your Character. Take care of your Character because it will form your Destiny, and your Destiny will be your Life. ~ The Dalai Lama

Finally, brothers and sisters, whatever is true, whatever is noble, whatever is right, whatever is pure, whatever is lovely, whatever is admirable—if anything is excellent or praiseworthy—think about such things. Whatever you have learned or received or heard from me, or seen in me—put it into practice. And the God of peace will be with you.

~ Philippians 4:8-9

We've suggested a few simple steps to help you change your language from negative to positive.

Learn to keep the door shut, keep out of your mind and out of your world, every element that seeks admittance with no definite helpful end in view.
~ George Matthew Adams

Step One:

Pick one thought out of the 60,000 you're going to think today. Out of your mind you can create what you dream of.

When I examine myself and my methods of thought, I come to the conclusion that the gift of fantasy has

meant more to me than any talent for abstract, positive thinking.
~Albert Einstein

All successful people men and women are big dreamers. They imagine what their future could be, ideal in every respect, and then they work every day toward their distant vision, that goal or purpose. ~Brian Tracy

<u>Step Two:</u>

Put your thoughts into words that accurately express your dream and desire and write it on paper.

Carry a note pad with you. When your creative being is sparked by one of the five senses write it down in the moment the inspiration exists.

Maybe you have a memory like an elephant, but you will never repeat that moment when the thought first came to you. It's too easy to forget the little details, so write it down.

You'll never experience this time and place again. Make the most of the present moment.

Goals allow you to control the direction of change in your favor.
~Brian Tracy

After you've written several thoughts down, turn your thoughts into goals and list them.

People with clear, written goals, accomplish far more in a shorter period of time than people without them could ever imagine. ~Brian Tracy

There are several schools of thought regarding creating and manifesting and whether or not you need to have goals, or if you need to write them down.

Some say that your Power Source, God/Universe/ subconscious mind, will bring about what you desire with no effort on your part.

"No eye has seen, no ear has heard, no mind has conceived what God has prepared for those who love Him."
1 Corinthians 2:9

It's your journey. Doing it one way or the other is probably not a deal breaker. But, it might be affirming to have a journal that you can go back and refer to.

Knowing that the Language of Success has made a difference in your life can in itself be life altering.

Use your life lessons and make a difference in someone else's life.

If you raise your children to feel that they can accomplish any goal or task they decide upon, you will have succeeded as a parent and you will have given your children the greatest of all blessings. ~Brian Tracy

Step Three:

You've got to feel it to believe it….breath it in and absorb it.

Feeling and longing are the motive forces behind all human endeavor and human creations. ~ Albert Einstein

The law of attraction says that like attracts like, and when you think and feel what you want to attract on the inside, the law will use people, circumstances and events to magnetize what you want. ~ Rhonda Byrne

Step Four:

Action is energy and energy is creative power. One of the keys to that creative power is using the right words which in turn accomplish the desired outcome.

Words have vibratory signatures. Words have vibrational frequency. Positive words have a higher vibration.

Higher the vibrational frequencies produce better outcomes. Higher frequencies attract positive energy. Positive energy creates positive outcome.

Shout it out, clap, dance, sing and embrace it!

Use clear and specific language which will direct the flow of energy that will bring to reality your dreams and desire.

All the breaks you need in life wait within your imagination. Imagination is the workshop of your mind, capable of turning mind energy into accomplishment and wealth.
~Napoleon Hill

Let's review:

Thoughts + words + feelings = action

Get a paper and pen. On the following pages is a list of positive words. Use these words as you write down your thoughts and goals.

Make your goals clear and concise, focus and be specific. Speak what you've written with feeling.

Yell it, clap your hands, get up and dance to it.

Engage energy's creative power into manifesting what you wrote on that paper.

All the breaks you need in life wait within your imagination. Imagination is the workshop of your mind, capable of turning mind energy into accomplishment and wealth.
~ Napoleon Hill

Prentice Mulford explained it well in his book *Thoughts are Things*, "Talk Creates Force," and the more who talk in unison the greater the volume and power (vibration/energy)of the thought generated for creating good. Be the positive force in your crowd.

Positive Word List

Absolutely-Abundant-Accept
Acclaimed-Accomplishment-
Achievement
Action-Active-Activist
Acumen-Adjust-Admire
Adopt-Adorable-Adored
Adventure-Affirmative-Affluent
Agree-Airy-Alive
Alliance-Alter-Amaze
Amity-Animated-Answer
Appreciation-Approve-Aptitude
Artistic-Assertive-Astonish
Astounding-Astute-Attractive

Authentic-Basic-Beaming
Beautiful-Believe-Benefactor
Benefit-Bighearted-Blessed
Charitable-Cherish-Clean
Commend-Comradery-
Connected
Conviction-Coupled-Cuddle
Curious-Delight-Distinguished
Each Day-Easy-Efficient
Elegance-Encourage-Energy
Enthuse-Essence-Esteemed
Exciting-Explore-Exhalant
Family-Fit-Fortunate
Fresh-Funny-Genius
Glad-Grace-Grateful
Gratitude-Grow-Harmony
Healthy-Hearty-Holy
Hug-I am-I can

I Create-I will-Imagination
Independent-Innovative-Instinct
Intuitive-Jovial-Kind
Laugh-Light-Lucrative
Meaning-Miracle-Motivate
One-Paradise-Perfect
Plenty-Powerful-Principle
Prominent-Proud-Ready
Refresh-Relax-Remarkable
Replenish-Respect-
Revolutionize
Safe-Sensation-Shine
Simple-Smile-Soul
Spirited-Spontaneous-Strong
Sunny-Surprise-Team
Thrilled-Today-Transform
Truth-Upbeat-Venture
Vigorous-Vital-Wealthy

Well-being-Wholeness-Wonder
Yes-Yes-Yes

There is no thought in my mind but it quickly tends to convert itself into a power and organizes a huge instrumentality of means.
~Ralph Waldo Emerson

There are numerous positive word lists. If you see or think of a word not here then add it.

Cause and effect is as absolute and undeviating in the hidden realm of thought as in the world of visible and material things. Mind is the master weaver, both of the interior garment of character and the outer garment of circumstance. ~James Allen

Thomas Edison famously said, "I haven't failed. I just found 10,000 ways that don't work."

Consider the possibility that those 10,000 ways were caulked full of 10,000 wrong words.

It's time to change your language. Writing affirmations is a good place to start. You can find examples of them everywhere.

Read them, pay attention to the positive words. Make positive words a habit.

Habit is a cable; we weave a thread of it every day, and at last we cannot break it. ~Horace Mann

The Language of Success…learn it, practice it, create it and live it!

Practice means to perform, over and over again in the face of all obstacles, some act of vision, of faith, of desire. Practice is a means of inviting the perfection desired. ~ Martha Graham, dancer & choreographer

This leads to the inevitable conclusion that if we wish to express abundance in our lives, we can afford to think abundance only, and as words are only thoughts taking form, we must be especially careful to use nothing but constructive and harmonious language, which when finally crystallized into objective forms, will prove to our advantage.

~ Charles Haanel, The Master Key System

Epilogue

By T.A. Laurin

It is unusual and quite different to think of ourselves as a Creating Machine while living the human existence. Influence outside yourself such as parents, teachers, religion, politics, education, and life experiences have shaped beliefs which define our life.

If we are not happy and feel like something is missing, it is simply out of habit and lack of information that we continue to remain on that path. Often, it is the discomfort or unacceptable pain of continued belief and behavior that prompts us to seek new direction. With this knowledge we can create a new destiny in a life of health, abundance, and happiness.

Just as our human engineering requires a heart and lungs to live, we have God given components that give us a success in life that will rock your world.

Yet, why is it that many people live their life with lack, disease, poverty, discouragement, and unfulfilled expectations? Why do most people live below their basic capability?

The formula to this process is simple to understand. You only have to seek after the creating knowledge and be responsible for the application of it in your life NOW.

This book explores one of the basic truths essential to understanding how to achieve a happy, abundant, and satisfied life.

The Creating Machine, Language of Success, is the first in a series of books that describe human beings as a creating machine. The Creating Machine describes our inherent God given capabilities, illustrates knowledge of spoken word power through example, and proves the ability to create a life with total satisfaction.

Without knowledge of these tools, you could be described as one having millions of dollars in the bank yet not knowing how to write a check. Whether we know it or not, the ability for us to create has been deposited into our account simply by being born on to this earth. Body, mind, and spirit together enable us to exist in the image and likeness of the Creator, and He has equipped us for the journey to live very well on earth.

One necessary and key element in the process to a successful life is our language. The simple, basic, or sophisticated words which we use every day are extremely powerful. The spoken words we speak have in them the power of life and death.

Choose your words wisely. Let them bring life to you. This book illustrates a simple "how to" approach with examples of people who have engaged the process successfully and made it part of their lifetime beliefs and habits. The benefit of your invested time to study this information will yield a high return just as it has for those illustrated.

Taking the time to understand this principle will give you access to a world within. If you choose to go within you will never go without. If you see your words as your wardrobe you can always be well dressed in life, and never again have to be naked and without. It is the authors desire that this book provide you an entry into the unseen power behind every word you speak.

As you recognize the principle of speaking strong positive words verses words filled with fear, doubt, and negativity, the universe is filled with energy just waiting to be manifested according to our spoken word.

To create is the nature of God. It was He who bestowed this ability unto mankind as a demonstration of His love.

The ability to create that which we desire, it is a key component to the process of cause and effect. What distinguishes humans from other creatures is our ability to create, free will to choose is our strength, whether we are consciously aware or not.

Wherever you are in life, at any age or in any place, it is available to you to seek out the process, and then you WILL find, followed by the result.

Look for the next book the in Creating Machine series to bring a deeper understanding in thoughts, actions, visualization, words, and faith to bring a fuller more meaningful life to you. It is the pleasure of the Creator to demonstrate the power of love through the life you can live. It is up to you, now begin to speak with faith filled positive words and watch your world become a light unto those who remain in darkness.

www.ingramcontent.com/pod-product-compliance
Lightning Source LLC
Chambersburg PA
CBHW071545170526
45166CB00004B/1560